little LULLABIES

I0877562

Special blankets to knit for babies—
choose the pattern you admire most; then relax and enjoy creating the perfect gift. You'll be knitting much more than just a pretty blanket. That's because Melissa Leapman's creations are as practical as they are beautiful. You can be sure each of these five designs will be a warm, long-wearing necessity for that precious baby!

MELISSA LEAPMAN

Melissa Leapman is a resident of New York City who began her design career by freelancing for major fashion manufacturers and yarn companies. Her ability to quickly develop fully envisioned garments put her skills in great demand. Through the years, Melissa's patterns have appeared in dozens of nationally known magazines, while her books and classes on knitting are consistently popular with the knitting public. To find additional knitting designs by Melissa Leapman, visit leisurearts.com.

LEISURE ARTS, INC.
Maumelle, Arkansas

terry

EASY

Finished Size: 32" x 45" (81.5 cm x 114.5 cm)

MATERIALS

Medium Weight Yarn (MEDIUM 4)
[3.5 ounces, 241 yards
(100 grams, 220 meters) per skein]:
MC (White) - 4 skeins
CC (Aqua) - 2 skeins
29" (73.5 cm) Circular knitting needles,
sizes 9 (5.5 mm) **and** 10 (6 mm) **or**
sizes needed for gauge

GAUGE: With larger size needle,
in pattern, 14 sts = 4" (10 cm)

BORDER

With smaller size needle and MC, cast on 113 sts.

Rows 1-12: Knit across.

BODY

Change to larger size needle.

Row 1 (Right side): K6, P1 (side border), knit across to last 7 sts, P1, K6 (side border).

Row 2: K7, purl across to last 7 sts, K7.

Row 3: K6, P1, knit across to last 7 sts, P1, K6.

Row 4: K7, purl across to last 7 sts, K7.

Both side borders of Body are worked at the same time, using separate yarn for **each** side. When instructed to slip a stitch, always slip as if to **purl** with yarn held **loosely** on **wrong** side of work.

Row 5: K6, P1, drop MC; with CC K1 ***(Fig. 3, page 15)***, [K1, YO ***(Fig. 1, page 14)***, K1] **all** in next st, ★ slip 1, (K1, YO, K1) **all** in next st; repeat from ★ across to last 8 sts, K1, drop CC; with next MC P1, K6: 211 sts.

Row 6: K7, drop MC; with CC K1, K3 tog tbl ***(Fig. 2, page 15)***, (slip 1, K3 tog tbl) across to last 8 sts, K1, cut CC; with next MC knit across: 113 sts.

Carry yarn not being used **loosely** along the wrong side edge of side border.

Row 7: K6, P1, knit across to last 7 sts, drop MC; with next MC P1, K6.

Row 8: K7, drop MC; with next MC purl across to last 7 sts, K7.

Rows 9 and 10: Repeat Rows 7 and 8.

Repeat Rows 5-10 for pattern until piece measures approximately 43½" (110.5 cm) from cast on edge, ending by working a **wrong** side MC row; cut CC.

BORDER

Change to smaller size needle.

Rows 1-12: With MC, knit across.

Bind off all sts in **knit**.

thomas

EASY

Finished Size: 36" x 45" (91.5 cm x 114.5 cm)

MATERIALS

Medium Weight Yarn (MEDIUM 4)
[3.5 ounces, 241 yards
(100 grams, 220 meters) per skein]:
- MC (White) - 5 skeins
- CC (Soft Teal) - 2 skeins

29" (73.5 cm) Circular knitting needles,
sizes 9 (5.5 mm) **and** 10 (6 mm) **or**
sizes needed for gauge

Cable needle

GAUGE: With larger size needle,
in pattern, 16 sts = 4" (10 cm)

STITCH GUIDE

CABLE 2 RIGHT *(abbreviated C2R)* (uses next 2 sts)
Slip next st onto cable needle and hold in **back** of work, K1 from left needle, K1 from cable needle.

CABLE 2 LEFT *(abbreviated C2L)* (uses next 2 sts)
Slip next st onto cable needle and hold in **front** of work, K1 from left needle, K1 from cable needle.

BORDER

With smaller size needle and MC, cast on 144 sts.

Rows 1-12: Knit across.

BODY

Change to larger size needle.

Both side borders of Body are worked at the same time, using separate yarn for **each** side. When instructed to slip a stitch, always slip as if to **purl** with yarn held **loosely** on **wrong** side of work.

Row 1 (Right side)**:** K6, P1, drop MC; with CC K1 ***(Fig. 3, page 15)***, slip 2, (K4, slip 2) across to last 8 sts, K1, drop CC; with next MC P1, K6.

Row 2: K7, drop MC; with CC P1, slip 2, (P4, slip 2) across to last 8 sts, P1, drop CC; with next MC K7.

Carry yarn not being used **loosely** along the wrong side edge of side border.

Row 3: K6, P1, C2R, C2L, (K2, C2R, C2L) across to last 7 sts, drop MC; with next MC P1, K6.

Row 4: K7, drop MC; with next MC purl across to last 7 sts, K7.

Row 5: K6, P1, drop MC; with CC K4, (slip 2, K4) across to last 7 sts, drop CC; with next MC P1, K6.

Row 6: K7, drop MC; with CC P4, (slip 2, P4) across to last 7 sts, drop CC; with next MC K7.

Row 7: K6, P1, K3, C2R, C2L, (K2, C2R, C2L) across to last 10 sts, K3, drop MC; with next MC P1, K6.

Row 8: K7, drop MC; with next MC purl across to last 7 sts, K7.

Row 9: K6, P1, drop MC; with CC K1, slip 2, (K4, slip 2) across to last 8 sts, K1, drop CC; with next MC P1, K6.

Repeat Rows 2-9 for pattern until piece measures approximately 43½" (110.5 cm) from cast on edge, ending by working a **wrong** side MC row; cut CC.

BORDER

Change to smaller size needle.

Rows 1-12: With MC, knit across.

Bind off all sts in **knit**.

timothy

EASY

Finished Size: $35^{1}/_{2}$" (90 cm) square

MATERIALS

Medium Weight Yarn (MEDIUM 4)
[3.5 ounces, 241 yards
(100 grams, 220 meters) per skein]:
- MC (White) - 4 skeins
- CC (Lt Purple) - 2 skeins

29" (73.5 cm) Circular knitting needles, sizes 9 (5.5 mm) **and** 10 (6 mm) **or** sizes needed for gauge

GAUGE: With larger size needle, in pattern, 17 sts = 4" (10 cm)

BORDER

With smaller size needle and MC, cast on 151 sts.

Rows 1-12: Knit across.

BODY

Change to larger size needle.

Both side borders of Body are worked at the same time, using separate yarn for **each** side. When instructed to slip a stitch, always slip as if to **purl** with yarn held **loosely** on **wrong** side of work.

Row 1 (Right side)**:** K6, P1 (side border), drop MC; with CC K1 ***(Fig. 3, page 15)***, (slip 1, K1) across to last 7 sts, drop CC; with next MC P1, K6 (side border).

Row 2: K7, drop MC; with CC K1, (slip 1, K1) across to last 7 sts, drop CC; with next MC K7.

Carry yarn not being used **loosely** along the wrong side edge of side border.

Row 3: K6, P1, knit across to last 7 sts, drop MC; with next MC P1, K6.

Row 4: K7, drop MC; with next MC knit across.

Row 5: K6, P1, drop MC; with CC K1, (slip 1, K1) across to last 7 sts, drop CC; with next MC P1, K6.

Repeat Rows 2-5 for pattern until piece measures approximately 34" (86.5 cm) from cast on edge, ending by working Row 2; cut CC.

BORDER

Change to smaller size needle.

Rows 1-12: With MC, knit across.

Bind off all sts in **knit**.

toni

EASY

Finished Size: 36" (91.5 cm) square

MATERIALS

Medium Weight Yarn (MEDIUM 4)
[3.5 ounces, 241 yards
(100 grams, 220 meters) per skein]:
- MC (White) - 3 skeins
- Color A (Aqua) - 2 skeins
- Color B (Soft Teal) - 2 skeins

29" (73.5 cm) Circular knitting needles, sizes 9 (5.5 mm) **and** 10 (6 mm) **or** sizes needed for gauge

GAUGE: With larger size needle, in pattern, 16 sts = 4" (10 cm)

BORDER

With smaller size needle and MC, cast on 144 sts.

Rows 1-12: Knit across.

BODY

Change to larger size needle.

Both side borders of Body are worked at the same time, using separate yarn for **each** side. When instructed to slip a stitch, always slip as if to **purl** with yarn held **loosely** on **wrong** side of work.

Row 1 (Right side)**:** K6, P1 (side border), drop MC; slip 2, with Color A ***(Fig. 3, page 15)*** (K2, slip 2) across to last 7 sts, drop Color A; with next MC P1, K6 (side border).

Row 2: K7, cut MC; slip 2, with Color A (P2, slip 2) across to last 7 sts, drop Color A; with next MC knit across.

Carry yarn not being used **loosely** along wrong side edge of side border.

Row 3: K6, P1, knit across to last 7 sts, P1, K6.

Row 4: K7, drop MC; with Color B P2, (slip 2, P2) across to last 7 sts, drop Color B; with next MC K7.

Row 5: K6, P1, cut MC; with Color B K2, (slip 2, K2) across to last 7 sts, drop Color B; with next MC P1, K6.

Row 6: K7, purl across to last 7 sts, K7.

Row 7: K6, P1, drop MC; slip 2, with Color A (K2, slip 2) across to last 7 sts, drop Color A; with next MC P1, K6.

Row 8: K7, cut MC; slip 2, with Color A (P2, slip 2) across to last 7 sts, drop Color A; with next MC knit across.

Repeat Rows 3-8 for pattern until piece measures approximately $34^1/_2$" (87.5 cm) from cast on edge, ending by working Row 6; cut Colors A and B.

BORDER

Change to smaller size needle.

Rows 1-12: With MC, knit across.

Bind off all sts in **knit**.

tabitha

EASY

Finished Size: 31½" x 45" (80 cm x 114.5 cm)

MATERIALS

Medium Weight Yarn (MEDIUM 4)
[3.5 ounces, 241 yards
(100 grams, 220 meters) per skein]:
- MC (White) - 4 skeins
- Color A (Lt Purple) - 1 skein
- Color B (Soft Teal) - 1 skein
- Color C (Aqua) - 1 skein

29" (73.5 cm) Circular knitting needles, sizes 9 (5.5 mm) **and** 10 (6 mm) **or** sizes needed for gauge

GAUGE: With larger size needle, in pattern, 16 sts = 4" (10 cm)

BORDER

With smaller size needle, cast on 126 sts.

Rows 1-12: Knit across.

BODY

Change to larger size needle.

Row 1 (Right side)**:** K6, P1 (side border), knit across to last 7 sts, P1, K6 (side border).

Row 2: K7, purl across to last 7 sts, K7.

Both side borders of Body are worked at the same time, using separate yarn for **each** side. When instructed to slip a stitch, always slip as if to **purl** with yarn held **loosely** on **wrong** side of work.

Row 3: K6, P1, drop MC; with Color A K4 ***(Fig. 3, page 15)***, (slip 2, K4) across to last 7 sts, drop Color A; with next MC P1, K6.

Row 4: K7, drop MC; with Color A K4, (slip 2, K4) across to last 7 sts, cut Color A; with next MC K7.

Row 5: K6, P1, knit across to last 7 sts, drop MC; with next MC P1, K6.

Row 6: K7, drop MC; with next MC purl across to last 7 sts, K7.

Row 7: K6, P1, drop MC; with Color B K1, slip 2, (K4, slip 2) across to last 8 sts, K1, drop Color B; with next MC P1, K6.

Row 8: K7, drop MC; with Color B K1, slip 2, (K4, slip 2) across to last 8 sts, K1, cut Color B; with next MC K7.

Row 9: K6, P1, knit across to last 7 sts, drop MC; with next MC P1, K6.

Row 10: K7, drop MC; with next MC purl across to last 7 sts, K7.

Instructions continued on page 12.

Row 11: K6, P1, drop MC; with Color C K4, (slip 2, K4) across to last 7 sts, drop Color C; with next MC P1, K6.

Row 12: K7, drop MC; with Color C K4, (slip 2, K4) across to last 7 sts, cut Color C; with next MC K7.

Row 13: K6, P1, knit across to last 7 sts, drop MC; with next MC P1, K6.

Row 14: K7, drop MC; with next MC purl across to last 7 sts, K7.

Row 15: K6, P1, drop MC; with Color A K1, slip 2, (K4, slip 2) across to last 8 sts, K1, drop Color A; with next MC P1, K6.

Row 16: K7, drop MC; with Color A K1, slip 2, (K4, slip 2) across to last 8 sts, K1, cut Color A; with next MC K7.

Row 17: K6, P1, knit across to last 7 sts, drop MC; with next MC P1, K6.

Row 18: K7, drop MC; with next MC purl across to last 7 sts, K7.

Row 19: K6, P1, drop MC; with Color B K4, (slip 2, K4) across to last 7 sts, drop Color B; with next MC P1, K6.

Row 20: K7, drop MC; with Color B K4, (slip 2, K4) across to last 7 sts, cut Color B; with next MC K7.

Row 21: K6, P1, knit across to last 7 sts, drop MC; with next MC P1, K6.

Row 22: K7, drop MC; with next MC purl across to last 7 sts, K7.

Row 23: K6, P1, drop MC; with Color C K1, slip 2, (K4, slip 2) across to last 8 sts, K1, drop Color C; with next MC P1, K6.

Row 24: K7, drop MC; with Color C K1, slip 2, (K4, slip 2) across to last 8 sts, K1, cut Color C; with next MC K7.

Row 25: K6, P1, knit across to last 7 sts, drop MC; with next MC P1, K6.

Row 26: K7, drop MC; with next MC purl across to last 7 sts, K7.

Repeat Rows 3-26 for pattern until piece measures approximately 43½" (110.5 cm) from cast on edge, ending by working a **wrong** side MC row.

BORDER

Change to smaller size needle.

Rows 1-12: With MC, knit across.

Bind off all sts in **knit**.

general instructions

ABBREVIATIONS

C2L	Cable 2 Left
C2R	Cable 2 Right
CC	Contrasting Color
cm	centimeters
K	knit
MC	Main Color
mm	millimeters
P	purl
st(s)	stitch(es)
tbl	through back loop(s)
tog	together
YO	yarn over

★ — work instructions following ★ as many **more** times as indicated in addition to the first time.

( ) or [ ] — work enclosed instructions **as many** times as specified by the number immediately following **or** work all enclosed instructions in the stitch indicated **or** contains explanatory remarks.

colon (:) — the number given after a colon at the end of a row denotes the number of stitches you should have on that row.

GAUGE

Exact gauge is essential for proper size. Before beginning your Afghan, make a sample swatch in the yarn and needle specified. After completing the swatch, measure it, counting your stitches carefully. If your swatch is larger or smaller than specified, **make another, changing needle size to get the correct gauge**. Keep trying until you find the size needle that will give you the specified gauge. Once proper gauge is obtained, measure width of Afghan approximately every 3" (7.5 cm) to be sure gauge remains consistent.

KNIT TERMINOLOGY		
UNITED STATES		**INTERNATIONAL**
gauge	=	tension
bind off	=	cast off
yarn over (YO)	=	yarn forward (yfwd) **or** yarn around needle (yrn)

BEGINNER	Projects for first-time knitters using basic knit and purl stitches. Minimal shaping.
EASY	Projects using basic stitches, repetitive stitch patterns, simple color changes, and simple shaping and finishing.
INTERMEDIATE	Projects with a variety of stitches, such as basic cables and lace, simple intarsia, double-pointed needles and knitting in the round needle techniques, mid-level shaping and finishing.
EXPERIENCED	Projects using advanced techniques and stitches, such as short rows, fair isle, more intricate intarsia, cables, lace patterns, and numerous color changes.

HINTS

Good finishing techniques make a big difference in the quality of your completed Afghan. Do not tie knots. Always start a new ball at the beginning of a row unless otherwise noted in the instructions, leaving ends long enough to weave in later.

Thread a yarn needle with the yarn end. With **wrong** side facing, weave the needle through several stitches, then reverse the direction and weave it back through several stitches. When ends are secure, clip them off close to work.

YARN OVER *(abbreviated YO)*

Bring the yarn forward **between** the needles, then back **over** the top of the right hand needle, so that it is now in position to knit the next stitch ***(Fig. 1)***.

Fig. 1

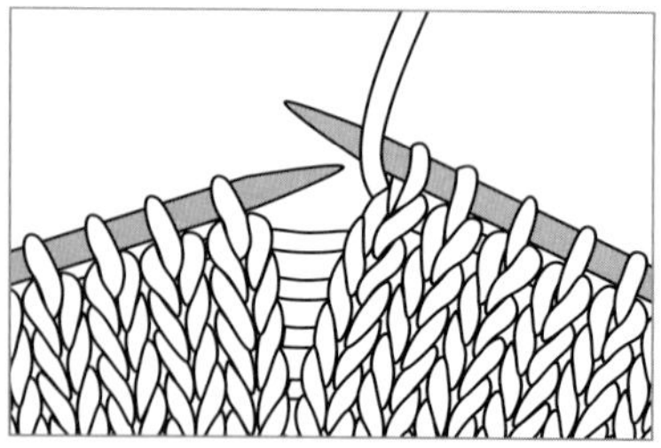

Yarn Weight Symbol & Names	SUPER FINE 1	FINE 2	LIGHT 3	MEDIUM 4	BULKY 5	SUPER BULKY 6
Type of Yarns in Category	Sock, Fingering Baby	Sport, Baby	DK, Light Worsted	Worsted, Afghan, Aran	Chunky, Craft, Rug	Bulky, Roving
Knit Gauge Ranges in Stockinette St to 4" (10 cm)	27-32 sts	23-26 sts	21-24 sts	16-20 sts	12-15 sts	6-11 sts
Advised Needle Size Range	1-3	3-5	5-7	7-9	9-11	11 and larger

KNITTING NEEDLES		
UNITED STATES	ENGLISH U.K.	METRIC (mm)
0	13	2
1	12	2.25
2	11	2.75
3	10	3.25
4	9	3.5
5	8	3.75
6	7	4
7	6	4.5
8	5	5
9	4	5.5
10	3	6
10½	2	6.5
11	1	8
13	00	9
15	000	10
17	---	12.75

KNIT 3 TOGETHER THROUGH BACK LOOP *(abbreviated K3tog tbl)*

Insert the right needle into the **back** of the first three stitches on the left needle ***(Fig. 2)***, then **knit** them together as if they were one stitch.

Fig. 2

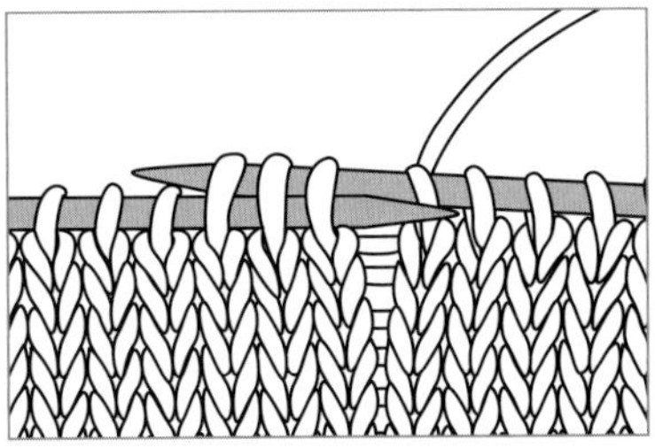

CHANGING COLORS

When changing colors, always pick up the new color yarn from beneath the dropped yarn and keep the color that has just been worked to the left of the new yarn ***(Fig. 3)***. This will prevent holes in the finished afghan. Take extra care to keep your tension even. Cut yarn when no longer needed.

Fig. 3

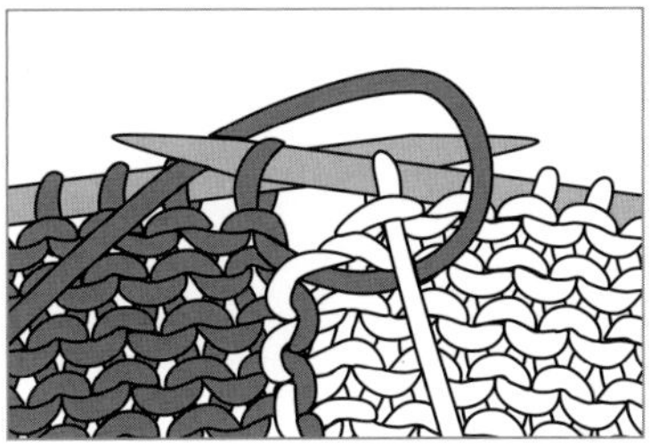

We have made every effort to ensure that these instructions are accurate and complete. We cannot, however, be responsible for human error, typographical mistakes, or variations in individual work.

Afghans made and instructions tested by Susan Carter, Raymelle Greening, Sue Galucki, Dale Potter, and Margaret Taverner.

Production Team: Writer/Technical Editor - Linda Daley; Editorial Writer - Susan McManus Johnson; Senior Graphic Artist - Lora Puls; Graphic Artists - Katherine Laughlin and Janie Wright; Photo Stylist - Christy Myers; and Photographer - Ken West.

YARN INFORMATION

Each Afghan in this leaflet was made using Patons® Canadiana, a Medium Weight Yarn. Any brand of Medium Weight Yarn may be used. It is best to refer to the yardage/meters when determining how many balls or skeins to purchase. Remember, to arrive at the finished size, it is the GAUGE/TENSION that is most important, not the brand of yarn.

For your convenience, listed below are the specific colors used to create our photography models.

TERRY
MC (White) - #00101 Winter White
CC (Aqua) - #00045 Aqua

THOMAS
MC (White) - #00101 Winter White
CC (Soft Teal) - #10730 Soft Teal

TIMOTHY
MC (White) - #00101 Winter White
CC (Lt Purple) - #10317 Lt Purple

TONI
MC (White) - #00101 Winter White
Color A (Aqua) - #00045 Aqua
Color B (Soft Teal) - #10730 Soft Teal

TABITHA
MC (White) - #00101 Winter White
Color A (Lt Purple) - #10317 Lt Purple
Color B (Soft Teal) - #10730 Soft Teal
Color C (Aqua) - #00045 Aqua